We Wish You a Poopy Christmas

Fudgy the Poopman's Collection
of Christmas Classics
Made Crappy

written by Bonnie Miller | *illustrated by* Nicole Narváez

Ulysses Press

Ulysses Press
P.O. Box 3440
Berkeley, CA 94703
www.ulyssespress.com

ISBN: 978-1-61243-843-6
Library of Congress Control Number: 2018944078

Printed in the United States by Jostens through Four Colour Print Group
10 9 8 7 6 5 4 3 2

Acquisitions editor: Casie Vogel
Managing editor: Claire Chun
Editorial: Shayna Keyles, Renee Rutledge, Claire Sielaff

Distributed by Publishers Group West

💩 Contents 💩

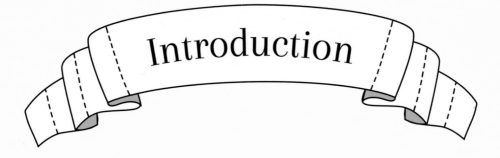

Introduction

Oh, hello! Howdy doo and a poopy Christmas to you! I'm Fudgy the Poopman. I'm here to share some of my favorite holiday poo classics with you. Butt, these aren't your traditional merry melodies; these are crappier, because Christmas for a poo is a little different than you're used to. You see, Christmas is the crappiest time of year for a Poopman, so we put a sh*tty twist on cheery carols and festive fables to make our own versions fecally fun.

Now if you can give me a moment to finish up here, come join me fireside, warm your buns, and enjoy my Christmas classics made crappy.

The Night Before Poopmas

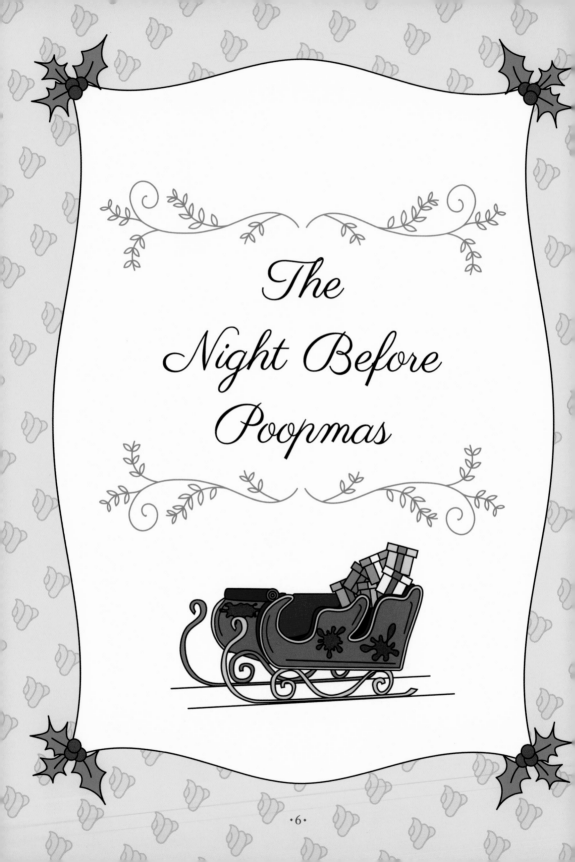

'Twas the night before Poopmas, when all through the loo
not a bowel was stirring, not even one poo.
The TP was hung by the commode with care,
in hopes that some turdlings would soon be dropped there.

The children were nestled all snug in their beds,
while visions of sugared prunes danced in their heads.
And me in my knickers, and papa in his cap,
had just settled in after two long, windy craps.

When out on the lawn there arose such a splatter,
I sprang from the bed to see who made the shatter.
Away to the window I spun like a flush,
tore open the shutters, and heard a gross mush.

There were mounds of manure on the new-fallen snow,
and all I could think was, "Oh shit! Oh no!"
When, what to my watering eyes should appear,
but a dung-covered sleigh, and eight pooping reindeer,
with a little old driver, so pissed and so ticked,
I knew in a moment it must be St. Nick.

Flustered and frazzled and full of such shame,
he cursed, and he shouted, and damned them by name:
"Dammit, DASHER! Dammit, DANCER! Dammit, PRANCER and VIXEN!
Oh come on, COMET! Come on CUPID! Come on, DONNER and BLITZEN!
You couldn't hold it for one night?! You couldn't hold it at all?!
Now toot away! Toot away! Toot away all!"

So up to the house-top their bums dropped more poo,
with the sleigh full of toys, St. Nicholas yelled, "Eww!"
And then, in a tinkling, I heard on the roof
the plopping and dropping of each little deuce.

As I plugged up my nose, and was sniffing around,
down the chimney St. Nicholas came with a bound.
He was dressed all in fur, from his head to his butt,
and his clothes were all splattered with doo and brown smut.
A ribbon of TP he had stuck on his back,
and he looked like a janitor exposing some crack.

His eyes—how they twinkled! His dimples, how merry!

His cheeks were like roses, he did not smell like cherry!

His droll little mouth was drawn up like a bow,

and the beard of his chin was not white as snow.

The stump of a pipe he held tight in his teeth,

and the smoke, it encircled his head like a wreath.

He had a broad face and a little round belly

that shook when he let out a fart quite smelly.

He was chubby and plump, a right stinky old elf,

and I dry-heaved when I smelled him, in spite of myself.

A wink of his eye and a twist of his head,

I soon knew this'd be a memory I'd dread.

He spoke not a word, but went straight to his work,

stole all our TP, then took off like a jerk!

Now laying his finger aside of his nose,

and giving a grimace, up the chimney he rose.

He sprang to his sleigh, to his team gave a good wipe,
and away they all flew like the dook-and-dash type.
But I heard him exclaim as he drove out of sight,
"HAPPY POOPMAS TO ALL, AND TO ALL A POOP-NIGHT!"

Rudy
the Red-Butt
Reindeer

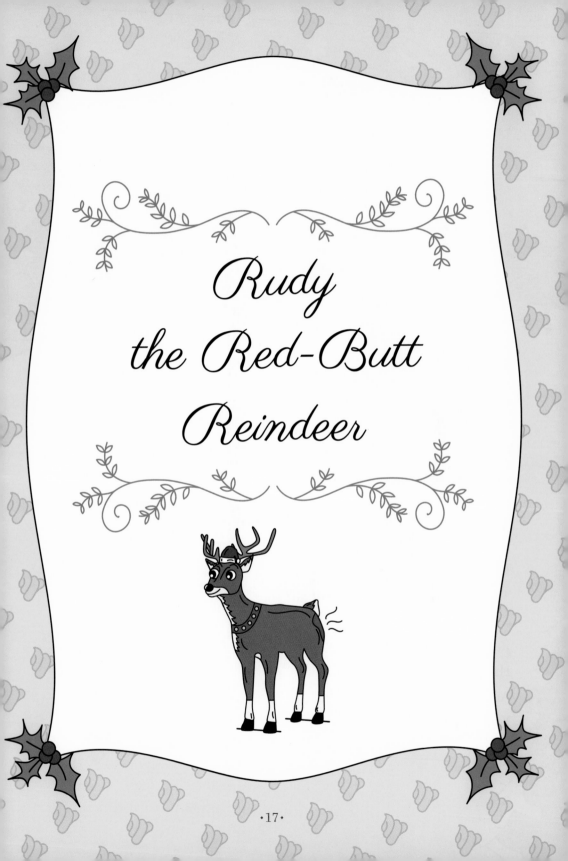

You know Dasher and Dancer and Prancer and Vixen,
Comet and Cupid and Donner and Blitzen.
But do you recall
The most flatulent reindeer of all?

Rudy the Red-Butt Reindeer
Had some very fiery bowels
And if you ever smelled them
You would even say they're foul.

Then one farty Christmas Eve,
Santa came to ask,
"Rudy, with your butt full of gas,
Won't you pull my big fat ass?"

Then how the reindeer fled him,
As they shouted out with dread,
"Rudy the Red-Butt Reindeer,
All your farts will kill us dead!"

The Twelve Days
of
Poopmas

On the first day of Poopmas,
my turd love sent to me:
A pinched loaf in a potty.

Pinched Loaf

On the second day of Poopmas,
my turd love sent to me:
Two twirly dumps,
And a pinched loaf in a potty.

Twirly Dumps

On the third day of Poopmas,
my turd love sent to me:
Three fudge babies,
Two twirly dumps,
And a pinched loaf in a potty.

Fudge Babies

On the fourth day of Poopmas,
my turd love sent to me:
Four coiled craps,
Three fudge babies,
Two twirly dumps,
And a pinched loaf in a potty.

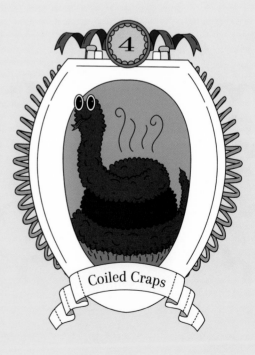

Coiled Craps

On the fifth day of Poopmas,
my turd love sent to me:
Five porcelain thrones,
Four coiled craps,
Three fudge babies,
Two twirly dumps,
And a pinched loaf in a potty.

Porcelain Thrones

Gassy Gusts

On the sixth day of Poopmas,
my turd love sent to me:
Six gassy gusts,
Five porcelain thrones,
Four coiled craps,
Three fudge babies,
Two twirly dumps,
And a pinched loaf in a potty.

Shits a Swirlin'

On the seventh day of Poopmas,
my turd love sent to me:
Seven shits a swirlin',
Six gassy gusts,
Five porcelain thrones,
Four coiled craps,
Three fudge babies,
Two twirly dumps,
And a pinched loaf in a potty.

On the eighth day of Poopmas,
my turd love sent to me:
Eight mighty mudslides,
Seven shits a swirlin',
Six gassy gusts,
Five porcelain thrones,
Four coiled craps,
Three fudge babies,
Two twirly dumps,
And a pinched loaf in a potty.

Mighty Mudslides

On the ninth day of Poopmas,
my turd love sent to me:
Nine berries dingling,
Eight mighty mudslides,
Seven shits a swirlin',
Six gassy gusts,
Five porcelain thrones,
Four coiled craps,
Three fudge babies,
Two twirly dumps,
And a pinched loaf in a potty.

Berries Dingling

Logs A-Floatin'

On the tenth day of Poopmas,
my turd love sent to me:
Ten logs a-floatin',
Nine berries dingling,
Eight mighty mudslides,
Seven shits a swirlin',
Six gassy gusts,
Five porcelain thrones,
Four coiled craps,
Three fudge babies,
Two twirly dumps,
And a pinched loaf in a potty.

Poopers Poopin'

On the eleventh day of Poopmas,
my turd love sent to me:
Eleven poopers poopin',
Ten logs a-floatin',
Nine berries dingling,
Eight mighty mudslides,
Seven shits a swirlin',
Six gassy gusts,
Five porcelain thrones,
Four coiled craps,
Three fudge babies,
Two twirly dumps,
And a pinched loaf in a potty.

On the twelfth day of Poopmas,
my turd love sent to me:
Twelve dookies droppin',
Eleven poopers poopin',
Ten logs a-floatin',
Nine berries dingling,
Eight mighty mudslides,
Seven shits a swirlin',
Six gassy gusts,
Five porcelain thrones,
Four coiled craps,
Three fudge babies,
Two twirly dumps,
And a pinched loaf in a potty.

Dookies Droppin'

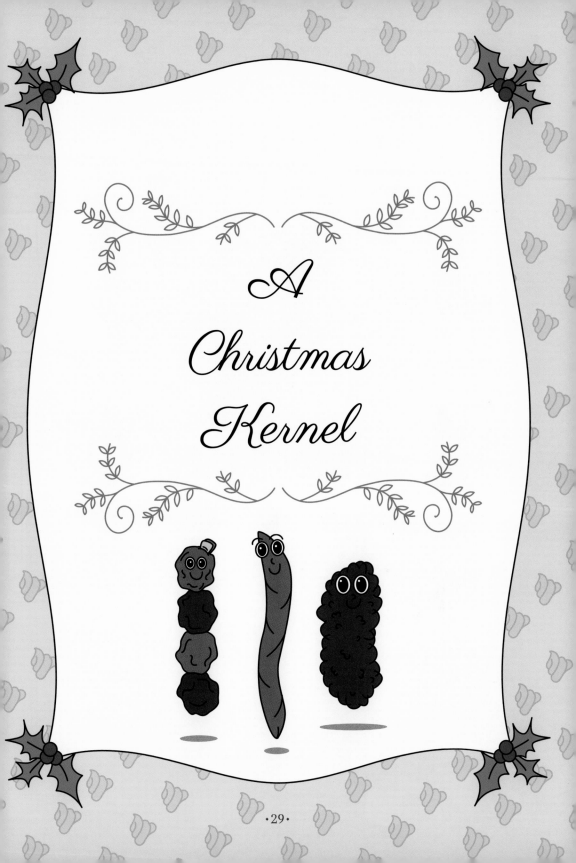

A
Christmas
Kernel

Once upon a toot, there lived a gassy old grump,
who just could not remember his very last dump.
For he was a smelly, old, constipated fool,
who called himself proudly, Ebetwozer Stool.
If you ever met him, you likely smelled gas
leaking from his bulbous, smelly old ass.
For Ebetwozer Stool never ate a fruit or veggie,
which is just what made him so downright curmudge-y.

But one Christmas Eve, after he pushed and he heaved,
three ghost turds emerged to recount his past deeds.
The first was as dry and as solid as could be
and from his ghost poop head, a single corn kernel you could see.
He showed Ebetwozer a memory quite old
that made his cramped colon a dilemma foretold.

For Ebetwozer's mother once fed him a green,
and he hated it so that he turned quite mean!
He spit and he spat,
and swore to her that
he would never again eat a fruit or veg.
And that, he said, was his final pledge.

The second ghost poop was smoother than the last,
and he showed Ebetwozer's friends having a blast.
As they played their charades, they pretended to toot
and held their bellies like fat rolls to boot.
Ebetwozer soon recognized that bloke—
he was indeed the butt of this joke.

Back to reality they flew in a flash
with a big thud and a toilet bowl splash.
While Ebetwozer longed to see what lay ahead,
he just as soon wanted to go back to bed.

The last ghost poop emerged to light the way
hoping that there was a mind he might sway.
For Ebetwozer was doomed if he did not reform:
His diet of junk caused his bowels to deform.

The poop showed him what some fiber could do
and how merry he'd feel if he could just poo.
Ebetwozer knew then that he'd surely die
if he didn't go drop some serious mud pie.

He dashed straight to the store and inside he found
laxatives, prune juice, and fiber by the pound.
He spent all of Christmas on the porcelain throne,
pooping and pooping as he groaned and he moaned.

All that dropping and plopping of gigantic yule logs,
and yet by some miracle he caused not one clog.
As he wiped up his crack one very last time,
he felt so amazing, like back in his prime.

A clean colon was truly the best gift to give
to himself and all those who could finally live
without the stench of Ebetwozer's rear.
And so on that Christmas, there were good tidings and cheer!

Silent Butt Deadly Night

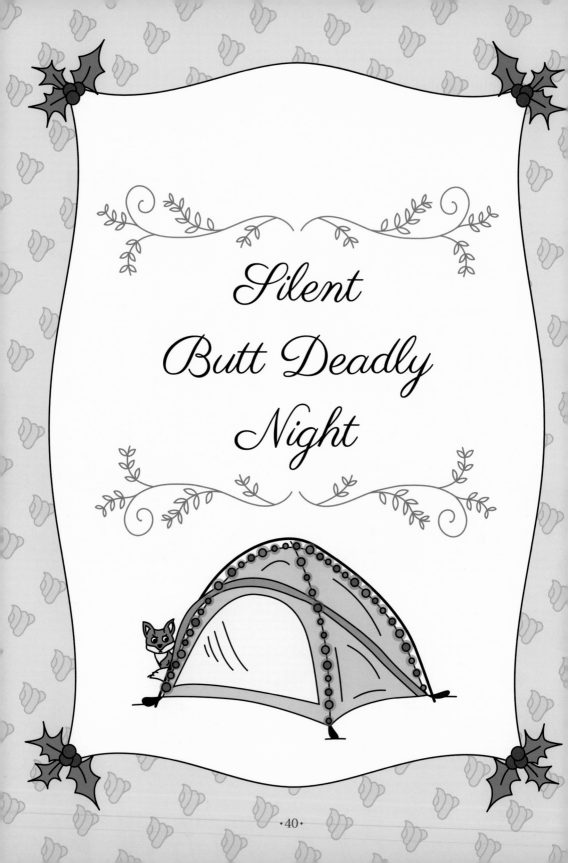

Silent night, holy shite!

All is fumes, all is not right.

'Round yon coals, farts afire.

Cut thy cheese so tender and sour.

Toot in silent peace,

Toot in silent peace.

Silent night, holy shite!
Noses pinched—stench quite a fright.
Gases stream from bowels afar
Hot wind rises to the North star,
Christ, the seam has been split!
Christ, the seam has been split.

Silent night, holy shite!
Son of a gun, those beans burn bright.
Radiate stench from unholy holes
With the stink of reaming disgrace,
Methane lingers from thy blast,
Methane lingers from thy blast.

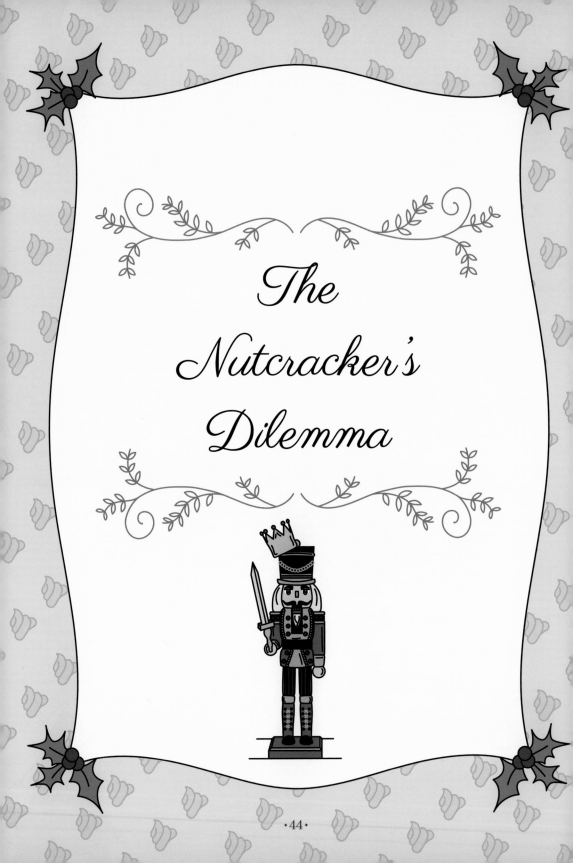

The Nutcracker's Dilemma

Egg nog with spiced rum,
Yule logs, and hot cocoa
all herald a season some
might find quite loco.
Most crazy, you ask? That creepy wood doll
with his huge, crunching mouth.
The nuts that he chomps—he gobbles them all.
And after he eats, the nuts travel south.

Nuts are very fiber rich
(they're filled with quite a lot).
Eat too many, you'll poop like a bitch
and spend all night on the pot.

So begins the story of nutcracker Ned.
He cricked and he cracked
every nut he was fed
until bursting was his poor GI tract.

Little did the humans know
that when they were not looking,
Ned's shiny cheeks did rosy glow—
he was alive! And to the toilet was booking.

Quick as a flash, Ned dashed to the toilet
where the Rat King was taking a poo.
From the sewer he came, to steal joy and spoil it.
To save Christmas, Ned knew what he must do.

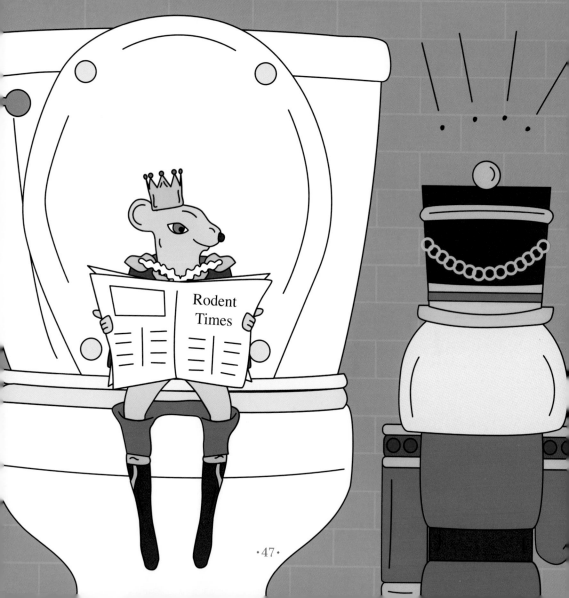

He brandished his sword and charged at the King.
The rat leaped from the throne and began to duel;
sword against sword, to the death they were fighting.
Ned struck the Rat King right in his belly, so cruel.

The victor shat, and he shit
'til his bum was quite raw,
then back to the mantle he flit
before any human knew what they saw.

And so the nut cracking carried on—
walnuts, almonds, hazelnuts, pecans—
until the Christmas season had come and gone
and Ned was packed away 'til the next one began.

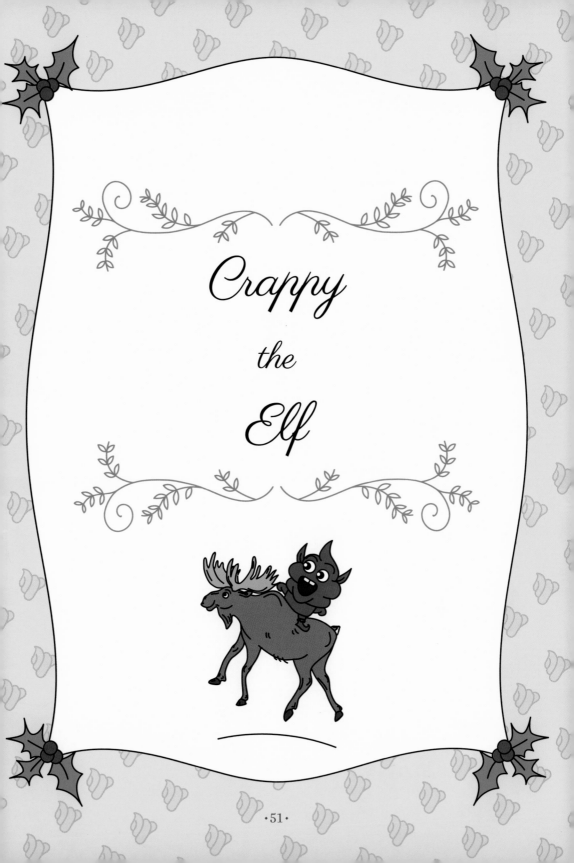

Crappy

the

Elf

One Christmas Eve night, Santa found his trousers too tight—
endless cookies and milk had his tum feeling not-so-right.
He scurried to Timmy Thompson's basement commode
and in the dead of night let his bowels fully unload.

A load so big that the deuce would not flush
so back to the chimney and to his sleigh he did rush.
Back to the North Pole he flew with a swoop
while the magic of Christmas gave life to that poop.

He called himself Crappy, and he knew just one thing:
he must find his poop father, for he was Santa's offspring.
To the North Pole he embarked on his journey
and hitched a ride with a trucker named Ernie.

From Kansas to Quebec, they drove and they drove
and warmed their toesies at night near a stove.
Quebec was where Ernie's journey would end;
the driver said goodbye to his newfound poop friend.

Crappy knew not where he should go from there
nor did it help that the townspeople would stare,
for they'd never seen a poop that had come to life
and he was chased out of town by a man with a knife.

On the banks of Saint Lawrence, he cried and he cried
and wished that quite soon, he might find a guide.
His wish did come true in the form of a moose
on which he rode atop his caboose.

But Crappy soon learned that this moose could fly
for he was half reindeer, and they took to the sky.
Over Newfoundland and Greenland they flew
until the North Pole came into view.

Crappy knew in a moment that he'd made it home:
the snow looked like white, billowy foam.
Soon the moose landed in Santa's front yard
and Crappy approached the elves standing guard.

TOY SHOP

REINDEER

He told them his tale of paternity
and of his lengthy journey.
They took him to Santa to see his reaction
and when Santa saw, he lost his foot traction.

Santa knew in a moment that his creation was cursed,
and drowned Crappy in the toilet, 'til he was fully submersed.

Conclusion

I hope you enjoyed this carefully clumped collection of crappy Christmas classics. Christmas for a poo is truly a joyous time for giving and going #2. From my crappy Poopman family to yours, we hope that your holidays are full of love and pinched loafs.

A Poopy Christmas to you, and to all a good night!